*The Gift of
Spiritual Direction*

The Gift of
Spiritual Direction

*On Spiritual
Guidance and
Care for the Soul*

WILFRID STINISSEN

Translated by Joseph B. Board, J.D., Ph.D.

Liguori
LIGUORI, MISSOURI

Translation copyright 1999 by Liguori Publications
Published by Liguori Publications
Liguori, Missouri
http://www.liguori.org

Original edition published in Swedish under the title *Andens terapi* by Bokförlaget Libris, Örebro, Sweden.

All rights reserved. No part of this publication may be reproduced, stored in a retrieval system, or transmitted in any form or by any means—electronic, mechanical, photocopy, recording, or any other—except for brief quotations in printed reviews, without the prior permission of the publisher.

Library of Congress Cataloging-in-Publication Data

Stinissen, Wilfrid 1927–.
 [Andens terapi. English]
 The gift of spiritual direction : on spiritual guidance and care for the soul / Wilfrid Stinissen ; translated by Joseph B. Board. — 1st U.S. ed.
   p. cm.
  ISBN 0-7648-0385-9
  1. Spiritual direction. I. Title.
BX2350.7.S7513 1999   98–55940
253.5'3—dc21

Excerpts from the English translation of the *Catechism of the Catholic Church* for the United States of America, © 1994, United States Catholic Conference, Inc.—Libreria Editrice Vaticana. Used by permission.

Printed in the United States of America
First U.S. Edition 1999
03 02 01 00 99 5 4 3 2

Contents

Foreword ~ vii

Chapter 1
The Spiritual Guide ~ 1

Chapter 2
The Relationship of
Caring for the Soul ~ 25

Chapter 3
The Dialogue ~ 47

Epilogue ~ 113

Notes ~ 115

Foreword

*M*ost recently, the demand for literature on care for the soul (spiritual charge of a parish) and spiritual guidance has increased markedly. This little book builds on four lectures on the subject, which I was invited to give at the Catholic priest seminary in Stockholm in the Spring of 1993.

The text, therefore, was originally directed toward a limited audience, with which I myself, as a Catholic priest, can easily identify. Now, after reworking and enlarging, it is being published for a broader public, I turn to both men and women, priests and others, who have some form of task that involves spiritual care. (For this reason, the changing forms "he" and "she" are used when the spiritual guide is mentioned.)

In his book, *The Dazzling Darkness*, Owe Wikström writes that if the Church does not pay proper attention to the need for spiritual guidance, it will be reduced to a religious institution which is caretaker for an interesting history and cultural inheritance (pp. 39–40). This is, in my opinion, the greatest danger that threatens the Church. Both its life and its radiation in the world are dependent on the members having a personal spiritual life. And in order that this personal life can be developed and enriched, there is need of concrete, personal guidance. Jesus' call to prayer for workers who shall reap the large harvest (Matthew 9:38) is today a call to prayer for good spiritual guides. There are unending resources for spiritual life in people today. But there are so few "workers" who understand how to use these resources properly.

In the Church, we need many well-equipped and experienced caretakers for souls. But in some measure, each Christian has a spiritual charge for the souls of their brothers and sisters. All of us should encourage, inspire, and support one another in the spiritual journey, say a good word, listen to and reinforce one another. And the marvelous thing is that what we give to a brother or a sister, we get back many times over.

CHAPTER 1

The Spiritual Guide

*T*here is a crying shortage of spiritual guides—a shortage all the more serious since, just in our time, there is a strong longing among many, indeed a crying out, for deepening and spirituality.

This search for spirituality is a consequence of, and a reaction against, the feeling of meaninglessness, hopelessness, and anguish which fills the world. And this in its turn is a consequence of God having disappeared from society. Without God, the human being becomes a problem for himself. "Without the Creator," says the Second

Vatican Council, "the creation is dissolved into nothing—yes, the very creation is darkened if one forgets God."[1]

Some seek help in yoga, Zen, or other Orient-inspired meditation. Sometimes they discover there new and deeper levels in their essence; they can experience a cosmic feeling of unity with everything and all. It can happen that such persons, driven by God's Spirit or through contact with a Christian friend, come closer to the Church. If they are lucky enough to meet a deeply spiritual priest, all is well and good. But it often occurs that they happen upon a priest who has absolutely no understanding for what they have earlier experienced, who speaks a completely different language, who reacts with skepticism up to and including irony. These searching persons are not seldom more spiritual than the priests they meet. And as priests represent the Church for them, they easily can draw the conclusion that the Church has nothing to offer by way of spirituality.

It is the tragedy of the Church that it is in no position to capture the large multitude of persons who are searching for spirituality.

Many, many persons are seeking a spiritual leader or escort and find none. I know that some make unreasonably high demands and will never be satisfied. But we cannot deny that it has become difficult to find spiritual guides who have time or, rather, *take* the time to listen, help, comfort, encourage.

In the name of honesty, I want to add that a person who sincerely and persistently looks for a spiritual guide will find one. An Indian proverb says: "When the pupil is ready, the teacher will appear." And in the tradition of the desert fathers, we find a well-known adage: "One abbot asks another abbot: Why have our spiritual fathers no more words to give? Answer: Because the pupils no longer listen."

But it is in any event our job not to let persons seek in vain.

Now it so happens that you cannot appoint yourself as a spiritual guide. You can put up a shingle with texts like "psychotherapist" or "notary" or maybe even "confessor," but you can't put up a sign saying "spiritual guide." It would sound grotesque. It is not the guide who invites or collects confidants, but the confidants who choose their guide. But many more ought to prepare themselves so that they *can* be chosen.

With the thought of just this preparation in

mind, it can be useful to mention some of the qualities that a spiritual guide should have.

Experience

By "experience" I do not mean experience of spiritual guidance, but experience of God. According to Teresa of Ávila (1515–1582), a spiritual guide should have three qualities: good judgment, experience, and learning.

> If it is not possible to get hold of someone who combines these three merits, it is the first two that matter most; for educated men, it is always possible to find someone to advise them if this is needed.
>
> What I mean is that, for beginners, learning is of little advantage if it is not combined with exercise of prayer.[2]

Saint John of the Cross (1542–1591) says something similar:

> It is a matter of great weight that the soul, which will grow in composure and perfection, pays some attention to the

hands in which it entrusts itself, for as the teacher is, so will the pupil be, and like father, like son—the Leader must in addition to being wise and discriminating himself, also have experience. Even if the foundation for guiding the spirit is composed of insight and discrimination, the guide will nevertheless not succeed in taking the soul farther on the way of the spirit unless he has his own experience of what a pure and true soul is.[3]

In our time, we do not speak happily of spiritual "leadership." It sounds too authoritarian. Furthermore, we know, or should know, that the real Leader is the Holy Spirit. We prefer the term spiritual "guidance." To "guide" is, according to the dictionary, to *accompany* and show the way.

> Do not go before me; I maybe cannot
>   keep up.
> Do not go after me; I maybe won't find
>   the way.
> Let us go together.

A spiritual guide is one who accompanies, who himself travels the way. He doesn't need to be a saint, he can have many weaknesses and defects, but he must live with God, he must pray. God must be "active" for him. In the words of Meister Eckhart (ca. 1260–1327): The God who was a *thinked* God must become in some way an *active* God.

One can describe the aim of spiritual guidance in different ways. One can say that it is the guide's role to teach his confidant to *listen to God's Spirit,* to be more sensitive. But how can the guide teach this if he himself is not accustomed to listening to the Spirit? Or, one also thinks that the spiritual life or the spiritual searching is aimed at *discovering the soul's center,* the place where the Holy Trinity abides. But how can we help discover the center of the town if we ourselves have only stayed in the suburbs? Or, one can speak of *awakening the sleeping life.* Through baptism, we are implanted in Christ, introduced into the life of the Trinity. But all this is often a sleeping potential; it belongs to our unconscious or our subconscious. It needs to be awakened, brought to consciousness. How can we do this if this life has never been awakened within ourselves?

We cannot, of course, waken the sleeping life in the other only through words. If only it were so easy. The sleeping life awakens only through contact with life which has already awakened. To guide a person presumes and means, therefore, a constant process of transformation in the leader. It is truly not only the confidant who gains from the guidance. The guide must gain at least as much. He cannot transfer life if he himself is not alive; he is forced by his confidants to take his relationship to God seriously. It is a great gift to be there as a spiritual guide for those who long for, who seek, who will live in relationship with God. If one takes this task seriously, it is impossible for one to stagnate. One must come to be developed, to be deepened.

Respect

By respect, I mean that one is deeply aware of the human being's value and worth. One does not play with humans, use them, bind them, or deprive them of their freedom. It is a great thing to be a human being, especially since God himself became human and Jesus Christ identified himself with each human being. When someone comes to us to confess or ask for advice, we should react as Elizabeth did when Mary came to her: "And why has this happened to me, that the mother of my Lord comes to me?" (Luke 1:43). It would be absurd to believe that one who is father, confessor, or spiritual guide is superior and stands higher than the other. It is not the spiritual guide who stands in the center, but the one who seeks guidance. It is him or her we serve.

Anthony Bloom writes:

> I believe first that you must understand that you cannot adopt a superior attitude, while the other has an inferior standing. You are not the one who gives, while the other stands there like a beggar who receives. It is not only that there is a complete equality between you, but even that the one who comes to you gives more than he receives....He makes you an offer, which is so great and generous that it well nigh should make us weep. The other gives in all humility his expectation and his trust. He reveals himself in all his weakness and fear, his failures and his guilt, in order to receive

help. An act of this magnitude shows such reverence for what is true, just, and human and for God himself, that we can approach such a person only with a feeling of worship and fear of God. It is the one who comes who gives most. We must remember this and stand in the place of a beggar, not of a rich man.[4]

We should always bow down deep inside ourselves when someone comes to confess. It is not just any person who makes a confession, but in and through this person, it is Jesus who confesses the sins of the person confessing. On the cross, he took upon himself the sins of all mankind and made a cosmic confession before the Father. In some way everything has already been confessed once and for all by Jesus on the cross. Each time a person confesses, he walks into this cosmic confession and lets it be present in his life. To hear a confession should always fill us with holy dread. Something of this dread ought also to be found when we, as spiritual guides, get ready for a conversation involving spiritual guidance.

Respect also means that one takes into consideration the personal path which the confidant is called to follow. There are many paths which lead to God. A spiritual guide who has himself found his "way" in the charismatic movement can be tempted to let his confidant go the same way. But it is quite possible that the charismatic movement doesn't suit him or her. To then accuse the confidant of lack of faith is deeply unjust. Each and every person has his own gift, his own charisma.

It is true that all must follow the gospels. But it is precisely the gospels which show many paths. For one thing, there is not *one* gospel, but four, and we know that each evangelist treats the life and message of Jesus from a personal standpoint and has his own priorities. One can follow Jesus in many different ways. One can, as he did, withdraw into the wilderness in order to be alone with the Father, or one can go out—as he did—and proclaim the message or heal the sick. Francis reads something else in the gospel than Ignatius does, and both are followers of Christ. The tremendous multiplicity of orders and congregations that we encounter in the Latin Church is concrete evidence that there are many different paths. Who am I that I should dare to place another person on my path?

A good spiritual guide is capable of seeing

the relativity of the different paths and forms of spirituality. He does not indulge a spirituality on the grounds that it doesn't suit himself. He only wants to know what suits his confidant. It is normal for a guide to believe most in his own way and that he can best mediate just that way. Likewise, it is also natural for a person to turn to a spiritual leader whom he thinks is on a path related to his own. But the really gifted leader is still the one who is open to all ways and is capable of listening to what the Spirit has in mind for just that person.

There are not only many different spiritualities, incarnated in different Orders. Each spirituality in itself is a theme with many variations. I can give my own Order, which I know best, as an example. We have within Carmel three known heroes: Teresa of Ávila, John of the Cross, and Thérèse of Lisieux. They all follow the same rule, about the same daily schedule, have the same "spirituality." And, nevertheless, what a difference! The extroverted, charming Teresa is not at all like the introverted John of the Cross. And little Thérèse is, in her turn, something completely new.

The more a person approaches God, the more distinct appears his personal, quite unique way. It receives clearer contours. His behavior becomes less and less a form of cliché, his violin acquires its own sound. The Book of Revelation speaks about a new name which is written on the white stone, a name which no one knows except the one who receives it (Revelation 2:17). This name expresses the person's unique calling, his own charisma, that which distinguishes him from all others. This name becomes more distinct the more you approach your life's goal. It becomes easier to decipher, both for the one who bears the name and for the one who has to guide him or her.

Nothing is as fascinating as being a spiritual guide for a cloister community which really "lives." Each time a new sister comes, a new register is taken out. In spite of the fact that all live in the same Order, even in the same community, hear the same sermons, and have the same abbess or prioress, no sister resembles any other. The Holy Spirit is endlessly inventive, it never repeats itself or plagiarizes.

For the third thing, respect means that one does not intervene lightly, does not conduct oneself as a superior who can give orders. One has to obey a superior, but there is no duty to obey vis-à-vis a spiritual guide. The guide most resembles a midwife. She must be a master in "maieutic" (the art of birth). "Maieutic" is, as is known, Socrates' method to "give birth" to the thoughts of listeners through posing questions. A midwife does not herself give life; she aids the woman giving birth and seeks to ease the birth. A spiritual guide does the same. He cannot himself bring about life, but he can create a climate, an atmosphere that facilitates the birth of the new life. To actively want to hurry up the birth of the new person is risky. "A time to be born...," says the Preacher (Ecclesiastes 3:2). To try to bring forth the new life before the time is come, or to demand more of the confidant than she is capable of, always prolongs the process.

In her autobiography, Teresa of Ávila gives us a typical example of how the spiritual guide's excessively high demands can have the opposite effect. She turned to the master Gaspar Daza, who with a holy—or, better, unholy—eagerness demands a radical transformation. Teresa writes:

> When I got into conversation with him, I felt the greatest bewilderment in the presence of such a holy man....He

began with holy decisiveness to lead me as if I were a strong soul, which he had reason to believe when he saw what kind of prayers I devoted myself to, and expected that I would not provoke God in the slightest way.

When I saw with what resolution he attacked the small sins I talked about and how I lacked the strength to reach immediately, reach such high perfection, I became confused, and when I noted that he treated my soul's concerns as if I immediately should rectify them, I saw concerns that it required much greater care on his part. Finally I understood that the means he prescribed were not suitable to heal me; they were designed for more perfect souls....

I truly believe that if I had had no one else to talk with, my soul never would have been improved. For the despair I felt when I didn't do as he said—and neither did I believe that I could do it—was enough to make me lose hope and give up altogether.[5]

By way of summary, we can say that a spiritual guide who always has a ready answer to all questions, who has a number of fixed principles which he squarely and indiscriminately applies in all situations, cannot be relied upon. He is perhaps a leader, but not a *guide*; that is, someone who accompanies and follows.

Mildness and Firmness

As spiritual guides, we represent God to those who entrust themselves to us. Our way of being and conducting ourselves inevitably influences our confidant's picture of God. If we are hard, they will come to experience God as hard. If we are nice and tractable, they will come to experience God as a nice and harmless God. It really is a matter of taking God as a model (Ephesians 5:1), of playing God.

God is simultaneously father and mother. When God created man in his image, he created both man and woman (Genesis 1:27). That which in him is one, is divided in humans. It is never the man or the woman alone who is an image of God, but the man with the woman and the woman with the man. Only together can they be a picture of God's love, which is both mild and powerful. He is *misericordia et veritas,* simultaneously tenderness, mercy—and truth, constancy, a rock.

In God these two qualities constitute a perfect synthesis. In the middle of the tenderness, he shows strength, and in the middle of strength, tenderness. One can even say that the more intensively and strongly God acts in man, the more God also shows tenderness. "God wounds tenderly," writes Saint John of the Cross. "Holy God, your leniency and mildness are the first signs of your omnipotence," we pray in the Catholic liturgy.[6] So long as one has not been "stuck" and "burned" by God, it is difficult to grasp how such a power can be combined with such tenderness.

In a harmonious family, it is relatively easy to reproduce and practice God's love with its double components of firmness and tenderness. It is more difficult when one must alone represent both aspects of God's love. When the spiritual guide believes that it is necessary to show firmness on a certain occasion, there is always the risk that the confidant will experience this firmness as hardness and also that it is, in fact, hardness. When the guide then understands that he has been hard and wounding, he can easily go over to the opposite. The goodness with which he will make up for and compensate for his hardness can easily become sentimentality. Nothing is so fateful as this swinging between two extremes. The confidant will become completely disoriented when he constantly receives conflicting signals. To draw a person to you through goodness and friendship, and then push him away, year after year, is a certain way to break him.

To harmonize tenderness and strength in relation to the confidant is one of the guide's most difficult tasks. One does not need to have long experience in spiritual guidance in order to know that certain confidants can get on one's nerves. Spiritual guides need endless patience! One can be attacked by one's confidants and their ceaseless talking at all times. They can get a guide to experience the telephone as the worst of all inventions.

I remember an anecdote from the life of J.B. Montini (later Pope Paul VI), told by one of his colleagues. When he worked at the state secretariat in the Vatican, nearly every morning, he was accustomed to being surrounded by one of his penitents. She talked and talked, and one could see on Montini's taut, desperate face that he was doing his best to control himself and not burst out in rage. That he didn't read the riot act to this woman, when he was so irritated, was great wisdom.

To say something when one is irritated is almost always wrong. "Speak in rage, and you will make the best speech you ever regretted," Winston Churchill is supposed to have said. But I believe that Montini would have acted wisely if, in a moment when he was not irritated but completely calm, he had let this woman understand that it wasn't a good idea to take so much time from a spiritual guide. It is not to the advantage of the confidant if one only indulges his or her unreasonable demands. In this way, one contributes to an increasing self-centeredness.

The perfect synthesis of mildness and firmness is not really to be found on this earth. It is based on not only a rarely sound psyche but also a high degree of spiritual maturity. In the absence of, but hopefully in expectation of, this maturity, we must do what we can. What we can do is: (1) try to get a clear insight into the fact that both these two aspects of love, mildness and firmness, are necessary and complement each other; and (2) learn to know ourselves and find out which of the two aspects is dominant in us.

Am I the one-sided firm type who tends toward hardness, or, on the contrary, the mild type who risks falling into harmless niceness?

To a sound firmness belongs something so concrete as to keep the guidance dialogue within limits for a determined time. To place an entire afternoon at one individual person's disposal can appear to be generous, but is, as a rule, more likely to reflect a lack of firmness. Within psychology, it is an established rule that the psychotherapeutic dialogue shall not last over an hour. Often, it is limited to fifty minutes. The same could hold as well for a guidance session.

It is important to be able to set limits. In this way, one helps the confidant to prepare for the session, to concentrate himself, not to lose himself in endless chattering, and, not least, to take his guide into consideration. And the guide himself gets in this way the occasion to work in a firm way by amicably but decisively leading the confidant back to the subject or the kernel of the matter.

This firmness, also when it is a matter of time one has available, contributes to a stricter structuring of both one's own and the other's spiritual life. And structuring, plainness, clarity, are often what the spiritual life needs most.

To firmness also belongs constancy in the relationship. When someone comes to me and asks, "Will you be my spiritual guide?" it would be wise for me not to reply immediately. I should sit down and consider whether I can or should invest time in this person, whether I really want to engage myself, whether the person in question is not so unbalanced or neurotic that I can predict I won't be able to stay with them. Above all, I must ask myself whether God wants it and let the matter ripen in prayer. If I in the end say yes, it must be a proper yes, not yes and no. And once I have said it, there must be serious reasons for breaking off the spiritual guidance relationship.

For most persons, it is a short step to choose a spiritual guide and entrust oneself to him or her. They should be able to rely on not being dismissed at the first available opportunity. It can very well happen that after a time, we regret that we have become involved in this, that it is much more difficult and bothersome than we had thought. But to give in to our irritation, lack of patience, or despair, and curtly break off the relationship can have catastrophic consequences for the confidant. It can, furthermore, negate all of the good that we have, with God's help, attained, so that all our efforts in the past not only are fruitless but even destructive, and the last error will be worse than the first. There are exceptions to all rules, but in general it's a good thing to hold on, conquer the crisis, seek new paths.

Nor should we forget—this has already been said, but it bears repeating—that our way of relating ourselves to our confidant affects his/her picture of God. If we show that we can't be relied upon, it means for confidants that they cannot rely on God. If we disappoint, it is God who disappoints. Also, many persons bear deep psychic wounds. Many have felt deserted, not loved, not seen, as children or later in life. When they turn to us, and ask for spiritual care, it is often *also* in order to finally be noticed, and restored in their human dignity. And let us then not too thoughtlessly say that this is a wrong point of departure. Jesus constantly restored people who had been abased. If these people, after having given us their trust and then been accepted and seen by us, at the end are brutally abandoned, this can tip them over into total hopelessness.

To show constancy in the relationship is really a combination of firmness and mildness.

Firmness above all in relation to ourselves. We don't give up because a conflict arises or because we begin to tire of a person's difficulties. And mildness in relation to the confidant, who must be able to rely on our not breaking the contact because they dared to appear as they were, in all their wretchedness.

The demand for mildness, goodness, mercy, will not be experienced as being especially harsh *if* one honestly seeks God. The deeper the spiritual guide penetrates into the inner stronghold of the soul, the milder and more merciful he becomes. He then becomes more and more like Jesus, who said of himself that he was "gentle and humble in heart" (Matthew 11:29). The holier one is, the better one understands the sinner.

If we live intensely, if we are willing to sacrifice all for Jesus Christ, we are also constantly confronted with our weakness. We have a painful sense of the enormous gap between our beautiful wishes and ugly deeds. We recognize ourselves in the words of Paul: "I do not understand my own actions. For I do not do what I want, but I do the very thing that I hate" (Romans 7:15). If we ourselves feel a driving need of God's mercy, we are not inclined to judge or prejudge. Then we cannot break off the bruised reed or quench the dimly burning wick (Isaiah 42:3, Matthew 12:20). We know we are no better than our confidants, we do not stand opposite them as the just versus the sinners. We belong to the same group, to the same category. We are there, not only in the company of the saints, but also of the sinners.

One aspect of mildness is that one can suffer *with* the other, in the literal meaning of the word: We suffer and we bear the suffering together. Jesus "began to weep" at the grave of Lazarus (John 11:35), not because Lazarus was dead (He knew that he would awaken him to life), but because he saw Martha and Mary's pain and suffered with them. This co-suffering is something quite different from speaking words of consolation. Consoling words can be deeply wounding when they are spoken by someone who doesn't know what he is speaking about, because he himself has not suffered. It is all too simple and cheap to speak sublime words about transfer and patience to a sick person who day and night is plagued by intolerable pain when you yourself are healthy. Only those who themselves have suffered have any right to talk.

A well-known French Cardinal who lay on

his deathbed said to a visiting priest—it was one of his last words: "We speak beautifully about suffering. I myself have preached on it glowingly. Tell the priests not to speak about it. We don't know what it is."

To suffer *with* others is an obvious fruit of love. Parents suffer when their children suffer. They don't have to exert themselves to do that; they cannot do otherwise, for they love. The spiritual guide is a channel through which God's love streams to persons. He is a living witness of Christ's goodness. One should be able to adapt to him what Sören Kierkegaard said about his father:

> Through him
> I know what a father's love is,
> through him
> I have an idea of God's fatherly love,
> the only unshakeable certainty in life,
> Archimedes' firm base.

CHAPTER 2

The Relationship of Caring for the Soul

*T*he relationship between leader and confidant is not something that is unequivocal. The confidant can and has the right to give the leader difference in influence over his life. The leader's role also changes, depending on whether he has an official relationship to the confidant or not.

Three Different Ways

In his book *La grâce peut davantage* (*Grace Can Do More*), the abbot André Louf distinguishes between three different ways to be a spiritual leader:

> The first way is, in today's West, the most frequent one, and it can be called *spiritual advising*. It presumes a free choice by the one who seeks advising—a choice which is never definitive: at any time, one can change advisors. Nor need the choice to be absolutely unique: even if one is best advised not to have several spiritual advisors at the same time, it is not out of the question that on occasion, one could consult another advisor. In female contemplative cloisters, this relationship is more or less institutionalized by giving the sisters two kinds of Father Confessor, which earlier was prescribed by Church law, and which is now still usable: one ordinary, who often also functions as a spiritual adviser, and an extraordinary, who comes several times a year, and who also

can advise. This usually works without much problem. Teresa of Ávila was eager to give her sisters opportunity to question spiritual and learned priests and it suited her fine, as well, when one of these advisers visited the nunnery. She stressed over and over the importance of a competent advisor and even founded a male branch of her reformed Carmel just so she could offer the sisters good spiritual leadership.

Under these circumstances, it isn't a matter directly of obedience, in any event not one of dutiful obedience, even if it is in the nature of the thing that the person seeking guidance is disposed to follow the advice given by the person he turns to in trust. In the Catholic Church, and even in other churches where priests administer the expiatory sacrament (confession), it is important that both they and the confidants understand the division in the roles of the priest as Father Confessor and as spiritual advisor. The penance which the Confessor gives obviously should be received obediently. A priest should not take for granted that a person will have him as spiritual advisor just because he once made a confession with the priest. To pose many questions at the first confession as if were obvious that the penitent will come back and seek spiritual guidance is both indiscreet and naïve.

A spiritual advisor does not treat the confidants as his children or as inferiors. Rather, he is a follower on the road which the advice-seeker, because of his knowledge and experience, has confidence in.

> The second way one could call *spiritual pedagogy*. One thinks immediately of a novice master (or mistress) in a monastic institution. Perhaps it can even be carried over to the catechumen. Here the leader typically has a concrete task: to prepare for the monastic vows, to guide to a certain spirituality, to form a Christian disposition based on the teachings of the faith. The relationship is a typical master-disciple one. It is limited in time: when the task has been carried out, and the teaching done, each and all go their own ways.

> One places *trust* in a spiritual advisor because of his personal qualities; a spiritual teacher, on

the other hand, one *follows* because of his official position.

The spiritual pedagogue's role should, as a rule, be given priority before other relationships. Priests and advisors should be conscious of this priority and avoid any form of collision. To contradict the novice master gladly and often is for the Father Confessor in a monastic community an all too easy way, to keep your own position but do nothing to improve the spiritual life of the penitent. The teaching requires unity in order to be accomplished. If needed, the pupil can always at a later time adjust or correct what the teacher presented.

Finally, one can speak about a *spiritual father* in the strict sense of the word. We find this relationship principally in the Orthodox tradition. What is central to such a relationship is not the leader's talent but the confidant's humility and trust. Trust not foremost in the leader, but in God who—so to speak—rewards the confidant's humility by making the leader's word benefit his spiritual development. There is a grain of truth in this. God lets everything be coordinated for the best for those who trust in Him. However, such a relationship can, if driven to its conclusion, completely set aside the confidant's own judgment and reason.

Here also thoughts about the vows of obedience are likely to come up. Even if there are, in the lives of the saints, certain examples of such a "successful" vow of obedience, one ought in my opinion resolutely refuse to support anyone who wishes to lay aside such a vow. There is no guarantee that the "spiritual father" or "spiritual mother" always carries out God's will. Among the Orthodox, some go so far as to maintain that one should remain faithful to his spiritual father and obey him even if one sees him sin. In the Western Church, there is more emphasis on the role of reason, sometimes certainly too much. But I believe that the spiritual advisor relationship will be healthier when the confidant himself also has a responsibility to look on with discernment what advice the leader gives.

To set aside the vow of obedience within an Order is something else altogether: then one lays aside the vow according to the rules and constitutions of the Order which limit the power of the individual. But to give up your whole life, on the other hand, without any reservation at all, into the hands of another person, can be to strain God. Jesus says that we are all brothers and that we shouldn't refer to anyone here on earth as "father" (Matthew 23:8–9). Can this not be interpreted to mean that in all relationships there must be a mutual responsibility? God's leadership for each individual person is always an interplay between receiving good advice from external sources (leaders, books) and listening to the internal leadership.[7]

Nearness and Distance

One of the most difficult things in the relationship between the spiritual advisor and the confidant is to maintain the balance between nearness and distance.

That eventually there should be a nearness, a personal relationship, between the guide and the confidant is obvious and is nothing to fear. The word "confidant" itself means that one has trust in one's spiritual guide and dares to entrust to him the most personal matters. Such a trust can only awaken a response. It is natural to be fond of a person who shows his trust.

The time is past when a spiritual advisor must be impersonal. Just juggling with abstract principles is of no great use. One can read these in books. It is much more the personal, spiritual radiance of the guide which helps the other person. And radiance presumes a certain openness. He must be able to invite another to himself, on occasion talk about his own experiences, positive and negative. It is not by putting himself on a pedestal, perfect and inaccessible, that he can inspire courage. He attains much more sometimes by telling about his own path.

A guide must show devotion to those who entrust themselves to him, so that they feel esteemed in a personal way. It is impossible to fulfill leadership out of duty alone.

An advising conversation is no job without a human relationship. The one who comes for advice can open himself only if he feels that the advisor is personally engaged, that he sincerely loves and values his confidant. When a Father Confessor gives absolution, he acts *in persona Christi* (in the name of Christ, on behalf of Christ). But the spiritual guide also acts *in persona propria* (in his own name): He shares with others his own experiences.

It is normal that a good spiritual guide should be esteemed and liked by those he leads. Teresa of Ávila writes something about this in her book *The Way of Perfection*, which she wrote for her sisters.

> Those who devote themselves to prayer and see that their Father Confessor is holy and understands them, will have great love for him and why shouldn't we love him? When we are attached to those who wish health for our bodies, why shouldn't we love those who work and exert themselves in order to promote the health of our souls? I think, on the contrary, that it has contributed to my spiritual growth when I like a Father Confessor who is holy and spiritual, and when I see that he has much to spare for the progress of my soul. For we are so weak that this devotion sometimes helps us a lot to accomplish great things in God's service.[8]

When this is said, it should be immediately added that there ought to be also a certain distance. Distance belongs to love. Love which really is love, and thus stands up for the *freedom* of the other person, is always a synthesis of nearness and distance. The guide should not bind his confidants to his own person, or himself to his confidants. The guide's only reason for existence is that he leads the confidant nearer to God. His finger must point in God's direction. But even if he does this, there is always someone who shows more interest in his finger than for the direction in which the finger points.

The risk is especially tangible when the guide and the confidant are of different sexes. The natural power of attraction toward the opposite sex—which is created by God and thus in itself something good—can influence an advising relationship in such a way that it hinders the relationship's real aim. This can happen both when men seek out women for advice, and—which is the most usual—when women seek spiritual advice from men. Women have by nature a greater disposition to attach themselves to another person. This is a part of their greatness when it is used in the right context. But it can also be a snare for her and for the man, if both have not consciously cultivated their personality.

When the guide notes that a woman in her thoughts is occupied too much with him, when she begins to talk about her great love and that she dreams about him, it is wise for him to display some reserve. Perhaps the confidant says: "You have helped me much in my life of prayer, but I don't know you at all. If I hadn't met you, I would have been lost. You are the most important person in my life and I think that we ought to talk a little more about our relationship and learn to know each other better." It is clear that the aim of guidance is completely ineffective when the emphasis is more on the relationship with the guide than with God. Here it is the task of the guide not to give in to a natural tendency to desire praise—something to which men especially are vulnerable.

He should show the firmness we have talked about. But a mild firmness. To brutally cast away a person who has just revealed how very much he means in her life can be disastrous. Perhaps it is the first time in her life that she's met someone whom she can really rely on and feel loved by. If the leader then coldly and tactlessly rejects her love or makes a jest about it, he can leave a wound which will never heal. The distance the guide creates must not give the confidant a feeling of being rejected again. He must clearly show that he stands fast in his care and love, that the distance is not a lack of love but a sign of greater love. It is this combination of nearness and distance which allows persons to grow.

Distance is also appropriate when the confidant takes too much of the guide's time, when she thinks that she is the only person who needs the leader's attention, or when she writes letter after letter with no thought of his limited resources. At that point, to create a bit more distance is not only a way for the leader himself to survive, it also teaches the confidant to take others into account.

Transference and Counter-Transference

One can't talk about the relationship of spiritual advising without saying a few words about transference and counter-transference. It is Freud above all who paid attention to this phenomenon, in spite of the fact that it was already known before him. Freud demonstrated that his patients were in the habit of transferring or carrying over to him the feelings that they, as children, had felt toward their parents. If the patient had had an authoritarian father, later in life he would meet this authoritarian father each time he came in contact with some form of authority. Each time, he experienced the same feeling of fear and powerless rage. But as it dealt with suppressed feelings, that is to say, feelings that one couldn't or didn't dare raise as a child, they showed themselves—when they finally came out—with a terrific intensity and vehemence. A person who in childhood didn't receive enough love from his mother can, later in life, constantly beg for love. At each encounter, he asks, with or without words, "Love me!"

Freud perceived that this transference to the therapist could be used in therapy. Since the feelings which come out in the transference have their origin in the past, the transference can create a bridge between the present and the traumatic past. Thanks to the transference, one can enter the past and render it conscious. One has a chance to influence it and, best of all, heal it.

But this requires great skill on the part of the therapist. Even the therapist has his psychic tangles; even he can have had traumatic experiences in his childhood which have led to certain reaction patterns.

If he himself had an authoritarian father, he will recognize his own father in the aggressive patient. One then speaks of counter-transference. If he himself had received too little love as a child, he risks being all too eager to answer the patient's need for love and thereby bind the patient to himself. It is extremely important that the therapist be conscious of his own frustrations, because in this way he can get some distance from them.

The therapist should stay neutral (which does not mean cold) and be sufficiently liberated from himself to accept the transference. One is dealing with the patient, not the therapist. If the therapist becomes angry when the patient accuses him of being a tyrant, and he repays with the same coin, he only makes matters worse. He thus accepts that the patient assigns him a role (for example, the authoritarian father) but refuses to play the role. Why does he refuse? Because he loves his patient, wishes him well, and wants to help him get away from the everlasting repetition of the same reaction patterns. When the patient hates him, he does not respond with hate, but remains calm and, if possible, impassive. When the patient declares her love, he doesn't take it for himself, and doesn't respond with the same type of love. The response should be a deeper love, one that does not bind but liberates. In this way he shows, not only with words but with his entire being, that there is another possibility than the one the patient is fixed on, that one does not *need* to pour out one's bile on his partner or drain him, that one *can* have a relationship which is both deep and liberating. So he helps the patient to examine his wrong way of dealing with others and gets him to conduct himself in a mature, adult way.

All this also holds for a spiritual advisor. He accepts the transference but refuses to play the role that the confidant expects of him. When the confidant declares her love for him, he doesn't need to brusquely and categorically reject it, which will only lead to a new trauma. He can calmly accept the love and say: "Thanks. Your devotion pleases me, it does not leave me unmoved. But how was it with your prayer—has anything happened since we last met?" He tries to get the confidant to return to the main point, and this is, when it is a matter of spiritual guidance, always the relationship to *God*.

It cannot be denied that there can also be found a bright and deep Christian "transference," which in itself has something to do with the mystery of the Incarnation. We can see Jesus Christ in each other, and above all in the priests. Jesus himself says, "Whoever listens to you listens to me" (Luke 10:16). Love and trust in him can be "transferred" to those who stand in his place—only it must take place with sound reasoning. Thérèse of the Child Jesus (1873–1897) writes to her sister Pauline and tells about her first confession when she was about seven years of age:

> They had said that it wasn't for a person I should confess my sins but for our Lord. I was completely convinced and made my confession with strong consciousness of belief. I questioned you right off if I shouldn't say to Abbé Ducellier that I loved him with all my heart, since it was our Lord I would talk with through him.[9]

Friendship?

Can one imagine that a deep bond of friendship exists between a spiritual guide and his confidant, a bond which does not bind but on the contrary, *liberates* to a more genuine life through a person becoming more himself when he shares everything with another? I use now the word "friendship" in its rich, full significance: a relationship where each one is to a high degree transparent for the other. We cannot deny that such friendships have existed and exist. One thinks of Francis de Sales and Jeanne Françoise de Chantal, of Teresa of Ávila and Peter Gracián, and Petrus de Dacia and Kristina av Stommeln. If such friendships have existed, it must be possible.

Saint John of the Cross describes in *The Dark Night of the Soul* how such a friendship functions; and at the same time he gives a plain criterion we can use in order to establish if a friendship is good:

> Some of these persons gladly entertain a selfish and bound friendship with each other on the plea of spirituality. But quite often these ties of friendship arise more out of sensuality than out of the faith's spirit. You can see this in that when this friendship is remembered it is not thoughts of love and God and love for him that are increased, but instead pains of conscience.
>
> For if this friendship is purely spiritual then the love for God grows

also with it. The more one remembers this friendship, the more often one is reminded of the friendship of God and finds happiness therein. As the one grows, so grows the other. God's Spirit has the qualities that it increases the one good along with the other as far as there is similarity and agreement among them.[10]

The initiative for deepened contacts often comes, as we said, from the confidant. The confidant perhaps feels great love for the spiritual advisor and wants to see it returned. The advisor must then be completely honest and not, out of regard for the confidant's need or not to make him disappointed, pretend to a love that he doesn't have.

Especially in relation to advice-seekers of the opposite sex, the advisor must be alert and not naively let himself be drawn into the confidant's feelings. It is quite possible that these will awaken a strong resonance within him. But it is part of his job to keep sufficient distance and self-control so as not to *follow* his feelings. Only then is it possible for him to take on the spiritual advisor's role, which absolutely gives God the foremost place, and he is clearly conscious that the relationship to the confidants has no other aim than to lead them to a richer relationship with God.

A male advisor who lives in celibacy, which is the case for Catholic priests, can many times be more naïve in the face of a woman's expression of feeling than one who is married. The married man receives, if he has a happy and deep relation with his wife, a natural balancing of his emotional life. It is obvious for him, or in any event ought to be, that faithfulness to his wife presumes that he maintains some distance in his feelings for those who entrust themselves to him. Among those who have chosen celibacy, their emotional lives are not harmonized in a similarly tangible way. But for the married man as well as for the celibate, it is simply one's faith in one's own calling that shows the right way to behave toward the confidants.

It is normal to feel, sometimes quite painfully, that celibacy is a sacrifice. One cannot live a celibate's life without a certain measure of suffering. Even if one lives close to God, and wants for him to be one's great happiness, there can be times when one lacks the intimacy and tenderness that a happy marriage can provide.

Celibacy does not change human nature. It would be unusual, even unnatural, if we should never feel the inborn longing for a woman that a man bears within himself. But it would be wrong just to give in to this attraction, to cultivate it, or get caught in it. Such a feeling or longing is each time an invitation to renew our vows, to repeat our original yes to Jesus Christ and to the Church, to relive our first love (cf. Revelation 2:4). "But recall those earlier days when, after you had been enlightened...you cheerfully accepted the plundering of your possessions, knowing that you yourselves possessed something better and more lasting" (Hebrews 10:32, 34).

Each time we are tormented by a feeling of loneliness, it gives us an opportunity not just to accept but voluntarily to affirm this loneliness, even to love it, because it makes possible a total undivided love for Christ. We are in fact not alone. The feeling of loneliness should always be a springboard to *reality*, and the reality is that he is always near us. In general, it is a good idea to be realistic and not cultivate naïve dreams that marriage always dispels loneliness. The great suffering of married persons is many times precisely loneliness.

For the married spiritual advisor, the sacrifice can consist in the fact that the exclusive relationship of the marriage excludes the possibility of a totally spiritual friendship with someone for whom one could feel a deeper spiritual union than with his marriage partner. But the fact is that we, who live as humans, must choose the one and exclude the other.

For the celibate, who did not choose the warm home milieu and the daily support of a woman's nearness, a spiritual relationship can, on the other hand, acquire greater depth and mean a more complete surrender.

But such a relationship or friendship is nothing that can be sought or evoked. It is a gift that God sometimes gives to those who have sought him wholeheartedly. This gift can be fruitful in relation to God only if the parties do not ask anything else from him.

Some celibates have never completely accepted and affirmed their loneliness. The result is often a certain hardness, sometimes a bit of bitterness. Then, it is difficult to communicate God's love. But those, on the other hand, who have understood the meaning of celibacy's loneliness can love it and give thanks for it.

For those who have not been happy in their

celibacy and its loneliness, it is highly imprudent to give in to a deep company with another person. This is for the most part a form of flight. As a rule, it is only after many years of happy loneliness that one is mature enough for such a friendship. "Everything has its time," says the Preacher, and everything must *be allowed* to have its time.

A decisive basic rule for the spiritual advisor is that he shall be awake and alert so as not in any way to seek satisfaction for his own part from his confidants, and that he is conscious of the subtle ways his egoism can seek outlets. Spiritual advising never is a matter of the advisor's honor and success. It deals exclusively with the confidant's growth in God.

CHAPTER 3

The Dialogue

Spiritual guidance takes place normally in and through a dialogue. We find a fine example in the gospels, namely in the dialogue between the rich man and Jesus (Mark 10:17–22). The man poses the question: "Good Teacher, what must I do to inherit eternal life?" Jesus replies by directing him to the Commandments and challenging the man to sell everything and follow him. This is very concrete spiritual guidance. The lead is given as a direct reply to the advice-seeker's questions. The desert fathers often were visited by their pupils who asked, "Father, how can I be saved? Give me a word." And the abba gave an abrupt and radical reply which the pupil could live from.

Our spiritual guidance should not always, in any event not immediately, be so "concentrated." To give a substantial word is meaningful only when the questioner is sufficiently open and prepared to receive it. Most people today feel they are living in an inner chaos. They carry lots of contradictory thoughts, wishes, motives. The basic emotion among many of them who seek spiritual guidance, and thus are driven by longing for a better life, is described as being torn apart. They are drawn in different directions: They want God and they want "the world"; they will live for others in love but they will not abstain from their own comfort; they want to pray but they also want to see interesting TV programs. To inject a holy word in this chaos can be profitless.

The first thing the confidant should be allowed to do is tell about his situation and describe his chaos. We find this also among the desert fathers. The young brothers came to their spiritual father, sometimes even daily, in order to reveal their *logismoi*. *Logismoi* means thoughts, but in its broad connotations: not only thoughts, but also wishes, feelings, passions, temptations—all things that move and haunt in head and heart.

The spiritual guide should be thankful if the confidant will and can talk about his or her inner chaos. This will be a point of departure from which the wandering can start.

Not all are prepared to be so honest. Some hide what is most "compromising," most humiliating, because they don't want to let the guide see how they really are. This dishonesty is often founded on a fear of being judged. This situation requires some patience. One can never "demand" a total openness. As trust in the spiritual leader increases, so openness usually also increases.

Others just *cannot* be open, either because they lack self-knowledge or because they are inhibited. Even then, it is important to have patience. An inhibited person is not helped much if the advisor says that they must be more open. Rather, what helps is an intensive listening which in the end entices forth the words.

To Listen Without Judging

The most important thing—and one of the most difficult—is just to listen. To listen without judging, either negatively or positively. Such an attitude has to do with the guide's own spiritual development. It belongs to a mature spiritual life to be able to receive each and every person with a kind of zero position. Not out of indifference for the other's well-being or woe, but out of trust in God.

What the confidant seeks is ordinarily not encouragement first and foremost—and when it concerns confession, not even absolution in the first place—but to exist as the person he is and be accepted as such. To reveal oneself is to take a terrific risk. Many feel ugly, dirty, miserable. When they finally get the courage—it really takes courage to show your nakedness—and overcome their shame, it happens almost always with trembling: Will my spiritual leader be shocked, will he still accept me when I speak the entire truth, will he break off all contact?

But the driving force is still a hope to be completely affirmed as the person we are or believe ourselves to be. Not so that we will always *remain* what we now are, but because we existentially know that we can go farther and be developed if we can begin from where we stand just now. We cannot shed our bad sides or liberate ourselves from wrong bonds if we don't first become affirmed as we are—just as we cannot give away what we have never owned. The confidants perhaps cry out for help to be able to change their lives, become mature, and develop, but the development must always proceed from a fundamental approval.

Each person longs to show himself to another person in all his reality, both the lights and the darks, and be "accepted" and loved as he is. "Welcome one another, therefore, just as Christ has welcomed you" (Romans 15:7). If we react with surprise, irritation, dislike, when someone trustingly reveals themselves, perhaps we only reinforce the confidant's evil suspicions: that he won't be accepted or that he *cannot* be accepted. Not to be accepted by his leader may cause the confidant to think that he won't be accepted by God. Such a big responsibility we have for the persons who place their trust in us.

When the guide thinks of himself as an ordinary, fragile human being, it is not always easy to immediately understand the significance that his role has for the confidant. He must learn to distinguish between his own person and the task he has. As a person, he remains a fragile co-traveler with his confidants. But at the same time, he will be, whether he is a priest or not, a vicar of Christ for those who come to him.

For a person who doesn't think he is accepted by God, it is difficult, even impossible—

if he truly seeks him—to accept his own self. To accept oneself is the point of departure for the spiritual way. Julian of Norwich (1342–ca 1416) goes so far as to dare to say: "When the soul is truly satisfied with itself, it is all at once united with God."[11] True sainthood consists in an unreserved yes to poverty.

But it is obvious, not excluding the guide's responsibility, that the confidant should be able to accept himself. In this as in all else, the leader must from the beginning show that he assumes and relies on the confidant's own resources. In each human encounter, we are right to try to have an attitude which makes clear our conviction that persons are not helplessly dependent on their psychic mechanisms. Our time needs to discover anew the capacity that the free will has. Perhaps one has never propagandized so much for freedom as now, but this freedom is actually a constraint subject to impulses, whims, and caprice. There is a deeper layer in humans where they themselves decide the meaning of their lives.

The acceptance should not exclude anything. Both light and dark *have to* be found there. It doesn't mean that one approves what is wrong. But here, in this first stage, it is still not the time to distinguish between good and evil. It is only a question of *letting* reality exist, to *let* it be what it is. If the spiritual leader does not do this, the confidant has perhaps no other way out than to do what he does for all others: play theater, camouflage what seems unacceptable—in other words, flee from the truth.

We priests often have an unhappy disposition to want to give advice immediately. We are perhaps well traveled in moral theology and think we know what is good and what is evil. When we see the way so clearly, why should we not show it, we think. We forget that if the way does not lead to the goal, *the truth*, it is for that reason no way. What we as spiritual advisors have to do is, in the first place, not to foster new behavior, but in concert with the true Spirit, lead persons to the truth both about themselves and about God. All saints and mystics stress that the building up of the spiritual life must be based on humility. And humility is just to accept completely the truth about oneself, the light and the dark. An unexcelled description of the truth about human beings can be found in the works of Bernard of Clairvaux (1090–1153): *Nihil sum sed tuus sum* (I am nothing but I am yours). It does not help anyone to discover by coming with moralistic pointers. Morality is a fruit of man's meeting with God, the meeting where he perceives his own emptiness and that God is his true life.

If we are surprised by what our confidants reveal, and find it difficult to understand how there is so much evil in humans, it is probably because we do not know ourselves and have not experienced a profound encounter with God. A saint always finds it difficult to understand his fellow human's sin. And he who was and is the most saintly never judged a man who honestly made known his sin to him.

To listen is more than to be silent. It is not enough purposely to let the other speak out while remaining silent at any price. It is truly already a beginning—and in fact not so easy to carry through as one might think. But among those who inside criticize and judge the confidant, the outer silence is a lie that violently collides with the confidant's attempt to be entirely true. To pretend a nonexistent understanding usually has no effect. The other knows intuitively whether he is really accepted or the guide is only using his technique.

The same thing happens if the guide shows a feigned accommodation as a way of giving the confidant time. It creates a better basis for trust if the guide openly and lovingly can say, "Today I have unfortunately no time to continue our conversation," rather than (with a patient exterior) sighing internally over the fact that the confidant never gets finished. Honesty, together with love, is the best of all situations.

Within certain schools of psychology, the importance of empathy, the capacity to live the reactions of other persons, is often emphasized. In Swedish, we have the beautiful word *inkännande* ("unfeeling"). A cold neutrality is no help to anyone. Empathy is possible only when I, listening, recognize in the other something of myself. I know that I am one with the other, for good or ill.

Unconditional Love

To break off the confidant's talking and your own listening by directing judgmental, reproachful, condemning words to him leads to no good. This is easy to see. But it is almost as bad to speak encouraging words, to exculpate, to cleanse. If you, in a conversation, when a person is opening himself and showing all his distress and his darker side, break off and begin to console by saying that in fact he isn't so ugly or that it is not as dark in his soul as he fears, this will scarcely lead to any deeper liberation. In the first place, he will become so frustrated when he is not allowed to speak out and will therefore not rely on our consoling words. He has not been able to explain *how* miserable and unlucky he feels. In the second place—the most important—we block the possibility of reaching a deeper level where the confidant will know that he is loved, independent of what he does and how he acts. Exculpatory words keep him fast at the level where he believes he must be fine, beautiful, attractive, in order to be loved. This is the conditional love's level: I love you only when you are loveable. By saying: "It's not so bad, you're fine, you are loveable in any event," we strengthen and reinforce his unconscious conviction that he must earn love, that we—and God—can love him only when he is completely unblemished.

What he basically wants to hear is not *you are less dark than you believe*, but *no matter how dark you are, I will love you anyway*. What every person hungers for is an unconditional love, a love without "because." This is the way God loves us, and it is this kind of love we have to mediate as spiritual guides.

God never says "I love you because you love me," or "I love you because you no longer sin." But: *I love you.* To love is his essence. That you exist is ontological evidence that he loves you. Everything he does is done out of love. When he creates you now, at this instant, he does it out of love. You are a fruit of his love.

If we don't mediate this, we fail both God and our confidant, but if we do it, the confidant gets the possibility to be completely reconciled with his whole being. Without this reconciliation, there is, as we have said, no chance for real development.

Our disposition to speak consoling, exculpating words can teach us something about ourselves. This disposition probably depends on we ourselves not resting in God's love, but still believing that we must earn it. If we ourselves have learned to know God's love, we don't even consider trying to convince our confidant that he isn't so bad. He can be as bad as bad; that still doesn't keep God from loving him. Nor us, either. One can be dark and beautiful at the same time: "I am black and beautiful" (Song of Solomon 1:5). Beautiful because of being loved.

To mediate God's unconditional love means grace for the spiritual guide himself. He cannot mediate it if he is not in some way anchored in it himself, and by mediating it, he becomes even more anchored. To listen, then, becomes almost a prayer. One listens out of a rock-fast certainty that one is loved, no matter what happens. We know that a third party is with us, and that it is he, the totally "accepting Other," who is the most important partner in the conversation.[12]

This limitless, merciful love is the meeting place between God and man. It is when man stands in all his poverty before God—and only then—that he finds his true worth.

When shortly before her death Thérèse of the Child Jesus concluded the manuscript where she recounted her life, she wrote:

> I know that even if I had all the sins one can commit on my conscience, I would, crushed by anguish, throw myself into the arms of Jesus, for I know how much he is fond of the lost child who returns to him. It is not because God in his mercy has kept my soul from mortal sin that I seek him in trust and love.[13]

To Mother Agnes, who would complete her unfinished manuscript, she adds:

> Say clearly, Mother, that even if I had committed every imaginable crime, I would always have the same trust, I would know that these many sins were like a drop of water cast into a glowing oven.[14]

The only unforgivable sin is not to *want* to be forgiven. Obviously we have to take into account all of the psychological circumstances which make this trust difficult. But it is also our task to confirm that trust, giving oneself over to God's love; this is an indwelling capacity in humans, and it is each person's calling to liberate this capacity.

To listen is much, much more than a technique.

Listening is the incarnation of God's merciful love, which not only does not judge, but also actively loves the persons exactly as they are.

To Recognize Man's Basic Longing

The confidant speaks in one or another way about his *logismoi*; that is, his thoughts, fantasies, wishes. After Freud, we understand that we are conscious of and can talk about only the tip of the iceberg. Our wishes, our motives, or the things that drive us, are for the most part a tremendously complex reality. The confidant can, by way of definition, talk only about what he himself understands about the iceberg. The rest is hidden to him. If we listen only to what is said, we will without fail be taken in. We must learn to listen also to what is not said, to what is hidden behind the words. Something that looks fine can in reality be quite ugly. A novice mistress told me that she was ashamed of her own tepid life when she saw with what burning eagerness one of her novices lived her cloistered life. It looked wonderful. But after several months, the novice left the cloister.

To make an objective judgment about outer acts is easy. But theories are not much help when we stand in front of someone who comes to us in trust. There are Christians who live a rather average spiritual life but never commit any tangibly serious mistakes, while others who live a deep and devoted inner life are never completely able to avoid missteps, even serious ones. Who is the greater sinner?

Just as something that looks fine can hide

something ugly, so also can something that looks ugly be an expression of something fine. It is this above all that we must learn to discover. There is no person who is completely evil. Sin has wounded man but not totally destroyed him. He is created for God, his basic longing is turned toward God. He is, like the Word, *pros ton Theon* (directed toward God) (John 1:1). This is indestructible. But this longing has in some way become blind. He doesn't know any longer where to direct it; he has lost his compass. Behind and under everything that humans in their concrete life long for is always this basic longing for God. They long for God, but seek him in the wrong place.

Evil is never a reality in itself. God cannot create any evil reality. Evil is always something good which has been distorted, which has lost its direction, which has still not found its right place, or which has lost its place. The error lies never in the longing itself—actually, one can never long too much—but in the fact that the longing is misdirected.

When a person is no longer conscious about his basic longing, when he has forgotten that his whole essence at bottom *is* the longing for God, he seeks desperately for something else which can fill his gulf. He throws himself on everything that comes his way, each time with the same question: "Perhaps you can make me happy, perhaps you can fill my longing?" And each time it ends in disappointment. That he feels himself to be so torn apart depends precisely on the fact that his basic longing is split up into a thousand small desires, that he turns to all possible surrogates instead of seeking the Only One who can satisfy him. Only after he has again begun to long for God "with his whole heart and all his strength" can there be unity in his life.

This doesn't mean that each desire that does not directly have God as its object is wrong. The important thing is that all desires be *integrated* in the great basic longing. The mistake begins when a desire goes its own ways, when it forms a tributary instead of letting its waters stream in the deep, broad riverbed that leads to the sea.

It is appropriate that we as spiritual guides not stare ourselves blind at what the confidant tells about his fantasies and desires, but that—behind and beyond them—he discovers his *basic longing* which is always a longing for love, a limitless love, the longing for God. When the guide sees this clearly, it becomes easier for the confidant to discover this for himself also. When he perceives that the many desires are actually a masquerading expression for a longing for limitless love, these lose a lot of their strength. When they are examined, freed of their masks, they become what they were intended to be, namely a part of the fundamental longing for God which resides in human beings.

The more a person's fundamental need for love becomes frustrated, the more he throws himself on all possible surrogates. That today's person is so restless, that he can't put up with an ordered, uniform life, that he thinks the whole time something must be happening, surely has its roots in this deep frustration. When the great love is missing, due to God's having disappeared and family life being so ill-used, one can only seek frenetically after something with which to fill the empty room. It is then extremely liberating to meet, in the spiritual guide, someone who himself has discovered the great love and who can also mediate it.

For this reason, it is inherent in the task of the spiritual guide that he himself live a life of prayer and nearness to God. He does his confidants a greater service when he sometimes gives them less time so that he himself can reserve time for prayer, than if he lets all his time be taken up by talk with them.

When love's "morning star" goes up in the confidant's heart (cf. 2 Peter 1:19), all desires begin to structure themselves and subordinate themselves to love. Chaos becomes cosmos, and the darkness becomes light.

Asceticism in Just the Right Measure

It is risky to exhort one's confidants to forsake their desires at too early a stage. To begin immediately to struggle for consolation is perhaps not so wise. Before Saint John of the Cross begins to describe the radical asceticism which he believes will set man free to receive God, he points out that man must be lit up with love for his Beloved. Without this love, it would be dangerous to give oneself over to strict asceticism.

Radical asceticism presumes a certain degree of mysticism. To wage a tough battle against desires that actually are clothed attempts to satisfy a fundamental, vital need for love carries with it the risk that one simultaneously constricts this fundamental need. The consequence that this need will seek new outlets is inescapable. Too early an asceticism mutilates persons. If efforts are exclusively aimed at forsaking, denying, rejecting, but not receiving, the Christian life will radiate hardness instead of love. Human beings cannot live in a vacuum. They are created for a loving life.

For someone who has once discovered love, the act of self-denial becomes obvious. Self-denial is no longer a naysaying to something alluring, but a yeasaying to something even more alluring—to choose the best before all else, to prefer love.

The criterion is *happiness*. If self-denial or asceticism significantly exceeds the measure of love one already has, the consequences are most likely sadness, depression, a feeling that life is gray. I say "significantly." It can, namely, be a good thing that the willingness to sacrifice is a bit greater than love, that it is—so to speak—a small step in advance and it tempts love to new heights. Such a sacrifice can awaken love; it is like a *small* piece of wood one throws into the fire. If the piece of wood is too large, it extinguishes the fire. A little self-denial can remind us that we have chosen the Lord, that we no longer belong to just ourselves.

With someone who has experienced a radical transformation, or with eagerness has begun a life of prayer, there is often awakened also a devoted will to sacrifice. It would be unwise of the guide to demand this. He should exhort to sound reason, to "order and judgment," as Saint John of the Cross writes,[15] but he shouldn't extinguish the burning fire. To sacrifice belongs to the Christian life (cf. Romans 12:1). Someone who has learned to sacrifice in external, perhaps banal things, will also be in a condition to abstain from his egoism in deeper and deeper things. The way of sacrificing also balances itself, since the spiritual development proceeds.

For someone who shuns all sacrifice, the guide is wise to try to inspire him to sacrifices that do not exceed normal human conditions, perhaps only to give a smile when one would prefer to show a sour countenance.

A self-denial that is in harmony with love, which thus does not run long before or lag far behind, leads to happiness. One has often misunderstood Jesus' words about denying himself and being mistaken about his life (Matthew 16:24–25). What I ought to deny is not the true "I" but the false "I," the old, unreformed person. The true "I" does well only by denying the false "I": egoism.

"But for me it is good to be near God" (Psalm 73:28). To be near God, not near to my egoism, to no longer think of myself, this is my happiness. It cannot be otherwise, since my real essence is to be open to God. "I delight to do your will, O my God; your law is within my heart" (Psalm 40:8).

All too often, eros and agape have been treated as enemies for whom it is impossible to live in peace with each other. Either you choose eros: In love for the other, you seek your own happiness, you think more about receiving than about giving; "you are mine," you say to the other. Or you choose agape: You think only about the other's happiness, you don't want to receive, or get, but give; you say, "I am yours." In actuality, eros and agape are siblings who need each other and who long for each other. Would I be able to make you happy (agape) if you didn't mean something to me, if there was not something in me which longed for you (eros)? Such a love is actually deeply humiliating. It is basically not love, but charity.

In a true love relationship, it is unthinkable to unilaterally only give or only receive. Mutuality is always just this teamwork between the two components of love.

We must teach those we have been entrusted to guide that love for God is not only an easily bought happiness but also a sacrifice, and at the same time teach them that it is not only a sacrifice but also a deep, true happiness. It is not wrong to want to be happy. God has created us to make us happy. The new *Catechism of the Catholic Church* (1994) begins with this sentence: "God, infinitely perfect and blessed in himself, in a plan of sheer goodness freely created man to make him share in his own blessed life."[16] God is our *beatitudo* (blessedness). To strive for *amour pur* (a love which is pure agape) is a risky business. "Love your neighbor as yourself," says both the Old and the New Testament. Give in order to receive; receive in order to give.

Only Love Has Creative Power

A spiritual guide loves his confidants. It would be noteworthy if it were otherwise. How would we stop loving those who put their trust in us when we ourselves are gripped by God's love?

We cannot love our confidants too much.

When it concerns real love, there is never any limit. We are always in debt (Romans 13:8). We cannot love too much, but we can express our love in the wrong way.

Only love has creative capacity. God is Creator because he is love. If we find it difficult with some of our confidants, we should pray for more love. We can paraphrase John 15:5: "Without love we can do nothing." And we can read Paul, in his song of praise to it: "Love is patient; love is kind; it is not irritable or resentful.... It bears all things, hopes all things, endures all things" (1 Corinthians 13:4–5, 7).

Our love, of course, should not be guided by sympathies or antipathies. We can often not regulate these ourselves, and we do not need to deny their existence. The question is what we do with them. We should not say to a confidant that we think she is wonderful when we actually feel annoyance with her, but obviously neither should we say that she is annoying. Love lies on another level. To love is—in this connection—to want the good for the other, independent of what I feel about her.

As our love always is or should be an incarnation of God's love, it must have the same quality, the same fragrance. And we know that what most characterizes God's love for us is mercy. Mercy is such an essential element of God's love that Saint Thomas Aquinas could write: "To forgive men, to show mercy to them, is a greater work than the creation of the world." The more we live according to the words of Jesus, "Blessed are the merciful, for they will receive mercy," (Matthew 5:7) the more true is the picture we give of God's love. The perfection that Jesus demands of us when he says, "Be perfect, therefore, as your heavenly Father is perfect" (Matthew 5:48) is the perfection of mercy. Luke has with great accuracy understood it in this way (Luke 6:36).

Some of the most important words in the gospels are: "Those who are well have no need of a physician, but those who are sick; I have come to call not the righteous but sinners" (Mark 2:17). We will never be able to completely extract all of the consequences of these words. The greatest poverty brings forth the greatest mercy, assuming that the poverty becomes acknowledged.

Don't our human relationships also show that the deepest love grows when we forgive each other? Jesus' life and death, which give us new life through reconciliation and forgiveness, is not a tragic necessity caused by human failure. It is, rather, a question of the completion of the work of the creation. God's mercy is most abundantly revealed precisely by his *act* of mercy for us.

The more we spiritual guides mediate God's mercy to others, the more we ourselves are opened to them. The mercy that streams through us cannot leave us unaffected. Perhaps we ourselves find it difficult to properly believe in God's love and mercy. But would it not be strange if *I* should be the only one in the whole world who doesn't have to take mercy into account? Still, there are so many who think—or "feel"—God loves mankind, of course, but how could he love a wretch like me!

Occasionally, we hear that in our time it is no longer meaningful to talk about God's mercy, since the consciousness of sin has disappeared. If one does not know what sin is, one cannot understand the meaning of mercy either. But all depends on *how* we preach about and mediate God's mercy. In the Church, one speaks occasionally a little one-sidedly about the forgiveness of sins, on how great it is to be freed from sin. The question is whether this means very much when one does not understand what sin is. Furthermore, to express "the forgiveness of sins" is not the entirety of God's loving acts toward humanity. What people of our time suffer from most of all is self-contempt, a feeling of inner lack, that they are not worth anything, of being no good. They feel that they are not whole. They experience themselves first of all not as sinners but as wounded.

Many persons are not "completely made" because of a lack of love on the part of the parents. The psychic constitution is damaged. Our preaching of God's mercy consists, then, in showing—through our words, but most of all through our whole way of being—that there is an infinite love, a sea of tenderness in which we can swim and which heals our wounds.

Over and over again, we must also maintain for our confidants that deep within them they bear something that is absolutely indestructible, which no wound can affect, and that, even if just now they cannot experience this inner temple, they will someday reach it. With Teresa of Ávila, we should remember "the soul's great worth and beauty" and that it is worthwhile to "devote all of our care to preserving this beauty."[17]

When one has become existentially conscious that God is love, one begins also to understand how frightful it is not to receive this love. Then the consciousness of sin begins to awaken, and then the forgiveness of sin also acquires a meaning.

To the degree that the spiritual guide knows, not only with head but also with heart, that he himself is loved, healed, created by God, he will mediate something of this to his confidants. If he doesn't have this inner knowledge, it is high time that he, through proper prayer, lets it breathe and grow. It is vitally important that he set about doing this, not only for his own but also for the confidant's sake.

To Speak

What has hitherto been said about silence and listening doesn't mean that one should never say anything. To be completely "non-directive" can possibly be right when it concerns a therapeutic relationship, but not when it concerns spiritual guidance. A spiritual advisor *has* actually something to say, but it mustn't be said too early. It *is* our job to teach, to mediate a spiritual tradition. Above all, it is our job to "individualize" and "personalize" the gospel, to adapt it to the confidant's concrete situation, not by making decisions for his calculation or dictating what decision he should make, but by pointing to certain basic attitudes which have their roots in the gospel.

I will suggest three such basic attitudes.

The secret of spiritual maturation is *never to be discouraged.* It doesn't matter if you fall, if only you raise yourself up again. "What do you do there in the monastery?" someone asked a monk one day. He replied, "We fall and rise, fall and rise, fall and rise again."[18] God's love is always greater than you can imagine. He never fails. You will sooner tire of sinning, said Teresa of Ávila, than he will tire of forgiving. *Deus semper maior.* God, Love, is always greater.

There is *nothing which can separate us from the love of God in Christ Jesus our Lord* (Romans 8:38–39). *All* circumstances and situations can be utilized (think about Freud's way of using transference!), all obstacles can be transformed into means. Even your sins can be positive by making you especially open to receive mercy.

It's a matter of leaving yourself in order

to find yourself, to die in order to rise up (the Easter mystery). A beginner is necessarily entangled in his egocentricity; it cannot be otherwise. The spiritual advisor has himself been there, is perhaps still there. But the development is such that nevertheless he becomes gradually free from his own self-centeredness. Spiritual maturity consists in the ability to truly love, thus to say "you" instead of "I." A spiritual advisor can give careful impulses to this exodus from oneself. How often people say, "I have no one who understands me, no one who listens to me." To that, we can reply: "Are you trying to listen, to understand?"

Each time we really help another to leave his old "I," we leave a little more of our own "I," assuming that we are honest in what we say.
Whoever helps another helps himself.

Discernment

I have already mentioned several qualities that each spiritual guide should have. There is one additional quality that I will treat a little more thoroughly, namely "discernment." Spiritual guidance consists in great part of this: to discern what is God's will with this particular person just now.

Saint Paul speaks about this capacity for discernment in his Letter to the Romans: "Do not be conformed to this world, but be transformed by the renewing of your minds, so that you may discern what is the will of God—what is good and acceptable and perfect" (Romans 12:2). To the Ephesians, he wrote: "So do not be foolish, but understand what the will of the Lord is" (Ephesians 5:17). And to the congregation in Colossae, he wrote: "...we have not ceased praying for you and asking that you may be filled with the knowledge of God's will in all spiritual wisdom and understanding, so that you may lead lives worthy of the Lord, fully pleasing to him..." (Colossians 1:9–10).

Each person has himself the duty and responsibility to discern what is God's will in his or her life. But most of them need help with this. The more a spiritual advisor is in harmony with the confidant's inner Leader, the Holy Spirit, the more sensitive antennae he gets to receive the Spirit's signals and the more his help comes to bear fruit.

How Does One Get the Capacity to Discern?

Those who are accustomed to open themselves to the Holy Spirit in *prayer* find it relatively easy to tune in if the confidant's words, thoughts, and desires are in harmony with him. A spiritual guide who does not pray is not as a rule interested in what the Spirit is saying, neither to himself nor to those for whom he has responsibility. He has his own intentions and principles which are undiscerningly applied to all.

As spiritual advisors, we should also devote ourselves to *lectio divina*, to read the Bible, slowly and in an atmosphere of prayer, with an open spirit which is receptive to what God, via these words, will say to us personally. As the Word is inspired, we become in this way close to the Spirit. We can be *dioratikoi*—those who see through things, both when it concerns the Word and our fellow man.

But prayer and Bible-reading are not enough. *Knowledge* is also needed. Knowledge about the rich spiritual tradition of the Church.

A spiritual advisor should know that there are different ways to pray, to live the Christian life. He has possibly learned a certain method of meditation, but if he knows no more than this about prayer, he can scarcely help others. The Church has an enormous spiritual experience. To not take advantage of this is an offense against those for whom we are responsible.

In our time, many feel drawn to a simple, silent prayer. They cannot or will not ponder a Bible text. They will abandon all thoughts and words and only "be" before God in what Saint John of the Cross calls *atencion amorosa* (loving attention). If we immediately stamp this as laziness or quietism, we risk blocking the Holy Spirit.

Others perhaps have sought contact with oriental methods of meditation and have learned to meditate with the help of a mantra. That so many in our day turn to Eastern prayer techniques is already symptomatic of the Church's inability to mediate its rich mystical tradition. If more priests knew something about Christian mysticism, there wouldn't be so many tempted to look in other places. But *if* they have sought and found something in Eastern teachers of wisdom, if, for example, they have learned to use a *mantra* (holy word), we should have sufficient knowledge of our own Christian tradition of prayer to show them that they don't need to search so far afield, that we have it, too, that many saints have prayed in this way, even that Jesus himself did it. Both Matthew (26:44) and Mark (14:39) point out that Jesus in Gethsemane prayed with the same words: "Your will be done." And Saint Paul maintains that the Spirit constantly repeats "Abba! Father!" into us (Galatians 4:6). Saint Francis prayed the whole night nothing but *Dio mio e mio tutto* (My God and my all).

If the spiritual guide doesn't know anything about this, if he has never heard about the prayers of Jesus, he can easily create confusion among those who seek advice. He can even give an impression that Christian spirituality is superficial, that it only deals with thoughts and words, that it doesn't have a feeling for mystery, and therefore is not open to apophatic methods of prayer, that is to say, methods where one is only silent in the face of the unsayable.

It is excellent to go through Ignatius' *Spiritual Exercises*. But for those who know *only* them, the risk is great that they will be treated as the one and only blessing. There are so many other ways which are legitimate and authentic. The guides should know something about them; otherwise they limit their confidants' freedom, instead of advancing it, and make themselves guilty of an ill-fated reductionism.

In spite of the fact that each person is unique, one can nevertheless discern three personality types. The Christian tradition has, through persons gifted with charisma, formed different spiritualities which fit certain "types." Each and every one's true personality corresponds to the way he is called to follow on his spiritual journey. The guide must not too simply think that he understands the confidant's personality type, but if he has knowledge, he can point out different ways, and then also help the confidant himself to ascertain which way he feels most at home with.

Periphery and Deep Layer

From which level does the confidant, by himself, speak? If he has read some spiritual literature, it can easily happen that he speaks out of his intellectual knowledge. He knows everything, but the knowledge is in his head and has no contact with reality. Some speak beautifully and spiritually but their lives don't correspond to the words.

This can be difficult to discern for an inexperienced guide. The confidant can be enchanting in his speech and show deep insights. This is not bad, but neither is it in itself any guarantee that the Holy Spirit leads him. Teresa of Ávila's three criteria for true prayer can also be adapted here in order to discern whether the confidant honestly is seeking God: love for one's neighbor, unbound by things, humility. With some simple questions, the advisor can obtain clarity about the confidant's disposition in these questions. And it is, as always, the disposition, the "temperament," which is decisive.

Does the confidant speak out of his superficial desires or out of his depth, his "heart"? Is there a genuine longing for God, or is the "spiritual life" nothing but a sublimated form of self-realization? Has the striving for holiness its roots in pride and ambition, or is it a work of the Spirit? Does one meditate in order to become calm and unstressed, or does one want to get nearer to God? Does one want to adorn one's "façade," or is one ready to die in order to let Christ live?

"What do you actually want, in your

innermost; what do you long for?" the guide should ask, over and over. He can do it directly or indirectly, according to the circumstances. By doing this, he can also get the confidant to perceive what is really worth longing for. "The desire for God is written in the human heart, because man is created by God and for God."[19] The external desires darken and block this inborn longing. But by placing the confidant in a position to confront the question as to what he most deeply longs for, the leader can help him to break through this block. Those who have a sensitive conscience will themselves look through the surface and the vanity in their desires.

False and Real Sense of Guilt

A spiritual advisor should be able to distinguish between a false and a real sense of guilt. A sense of guilt is false when it does not get involved with real guilt. It can depend on one having had a mother who was excessively strict and demanding: One was never good or clever enough, was always insufficient, felt like he always fell short. Or one has completely involuntarily made a mistake which has had difficult consequences for oneself or for others.

In such cases, to talk about God's forgiveness would be completely wrong. It is, rather, a matter of helping the confidant to greater clarity, to get him to see that the sense of guilt is unwarranted, illusory.

But it must take place with great patience. The false sense of guilt can be deeply rooted and it can be unwise to *immediately* say that it isn't genuine. The leader can begin by showing an attitude that expresses, "Even if you feel guilty and accuse yourself, God's love is so infinitely greater than everything—turn your gaze toward him and not toward your feelings." If the confidant then really directs himself toward God, he will come successively to see that the sense of guilt is groundless and therefore not constructive.

If, on the other hand, the sense of guilt is a consequence of real guilt, it should not be trivialized. The trust we give should not consist of minimizing the sin, but in that we maximize God's forgiveness. At the same time, it is our job to channel the sense of guilt in the right direction and let it develop into true remorse. Often the sense of guilt is more an expression of wounded pride than of real love. One is disappointed in oneself because one has not shown oneself to be as clever, fine, "virtuous" as one thought. "I regret my sin" often means: "I am sorry that I am not as good as I imagined I was." Such a self-centered regret is no proper "crushing of the heart."

In proper Christian remorse, one stands humble and contrite before God because one has not responded to his love or has responded to it with ingratitude. One has wounded love. But at the same time, one relies on God's limitless mercy. True concern goes hand in hand with susceptibility to God's forgiveness and contains therefore always a rehabilitation. Anyone who cannot believe in forgiveness is still sitting trapped in themselves. The humble person, on the other hand, knows that his own weakness, when it is recognized and repented, becomes an open gate for God. Remorse is not to drearily bewail our misery. Remorse is a positive force that means a desire for improvement and a trusting giving over to God. The guide must himself have seen this in his own life if he is to help to awaken it in others.

Self-centered remorse increases self-love and makes the sin even greater. Proper remorse, on the other hand, increases love for God; it permits the sin to contribute to greater love (cf. Romans 5:20). "Each sin has its corresponding blessing, because God is love," writes Julian of Norwich.[20]

The Superego or the Spirit

We also ought to be able to distinguish whether the confidant is letting himself be driven by his superego or by the Holy Spirit. This is closely related to the foregoing point. The superego is the part of the personality that checks and censors, a kind of crystallization of different forms of authority we meet in our lives. The more authoritarian the parents have been, the stronger as a rule the superego will be. A massive superego changes everything to compulsion. The entire Bible, which actually is one long declaration of love from God, is incorporated in the superego and becomes burdensome duties. The gospels become law, and as no one can keep the law (Romans 3:10, 7:15), it becomes a crushing burden. Instead of leading to freedom, the happy message leads to an even heavier sense of guilt.

It can be tempting for a spiritual advisor to give certain rules and prescriptions which function in his own life. He may himself get along fine by having a clearly established order for his life and his prayer which he follows in a disciplined way. He can then believe that his confidant functions in the same way. "Have more discipline in your life," he says. But it is possible that the other understands this as a new edict, which makes the burden of demands even greater. Perhaps, the guide should instead help him to a more untrammeled spontaneity.

A spiritual guide can very easily, without wanting or knowing it, ally himself with the confidant's superego. Even without being authoritarian, he can give nourishment to it by, for example, pointing to high ideals. Ideals can be inspiring and awaken slumbering energy. Augustine's words, *Quod isti et istae, cur non ego*? ("Why shouldn't even I be able to do what these holy men and women have done?"), have been a spur for many. But for others, it can be the contrary. Ideals can be crippling. One who already feels himself weighed down by the many imperatives of the superego can only interpret the ideal as still an imperative and a "categorical" one at that, which furthermore includes the entire existence. The spiritual life becomes still heavier and God still harder and more cruel.

On the other side, for some, the ideal can be a compensation and an alibi for everlasting failure. Instead of accepting the ugly reality, they flee and live in sublime dreams.

The goal toward we should help our confidants is not to reach sublime heights, but to be reconciled with themselves, with each other, and with God. To fully accept their weakness, even to be happy with it (2 Corinthians 12:10). Such an ideal is not damaging, not risky. It can be balsam for a person who is tormented by his superego.

Thérèse of the Child Jesus tells that in the beginning of her spiritual way, when she compared herself with the great saints, she felt like a little grain of sand alongside sky-high mountains. The ideals were unattainable. But it became her life's great discovery—a discovery she communicated to the whole Church—that the great happiness was just to be this little grain of sand, filled with trust in God's goodness and care.

Instead of *allying* oneself with the superego, it should be *neutralized* by the guide. This he does by showing, again and again, that God is so completely different from any authoritarian authority. God is goodness, mildness, mercy; even his so-called wrath—(proper wrath cannot be found in God: "I could not discover any trace of wrath in God," says Julian of Norwich[21])—must be seen in the light of love. It is nothing other than love's irrepressible, urgent attempt to awaken us. In the warmth of God's love, the superego eventually melts away.

Psychic and Spiritual

The talk about the superego reminds us how important it is to be able to distinguish between psychic and spiritual.

In the first place, it is clear that one cannot completely distinguish between the two. These two dimensions overlap each other. This has to be the case, because man is a substantial unity of body and soul, of matter and spirit. He is spirit incarnated, which means that everything in him is simultaneously incarnated and spiritual, "breathed through" (cf. Genesis 2:7). When theology says that grace builds on nature, this doesn't mean that nature is in the cellar and grace is on the first floor. No, grace permeates nature, ennobles it, elevates it, changes it. We find ourselves always in nature and grace at the same time. It is this way also when it concerns psychic and spiritual.

One-sidedness in this area can cause great

damage. Some see everything from a psychological point of view and expect everything from psychoanalysis and psychotherapy. Everything is psychologized. Others are overly spiritual and reject all psychotherapeutic help. Such guides will solve all problems with spiritual means, even when it clearly is a matter of psychic injuries.

That psychic and spiritual are united does not mean there is no distinction between them. The psychic is not the spiritual. A problem can have psychic or spiritual origins, but often the origins are both psychic and spiritual. It is not certain that one always helps a person by simply saying, "Pray a little more." It is possible that the person already prays a lot, but that the problem remains in any event. But is not certain either that one must immediately talk about psychotherapy. With a little common sense, we can find very simple means that contribute to greater psychic balance or help to heal psychic wounds—for example, relaxation, living in the present, being completely present in what you are doing ("reality therapy"), avoiding stress, having contact with nature, watching for burnout, living with positive thoughts, friendship; self-acceptance of your psychic wounds already begins the healing.

In other cases, it is necessary to have recourse to expertise. But not just any old psychotherapist. To look up some addresses in the telephone directory is risky. Some spend a fortune on psychotherapy without being much better for it. Many therapists are too one-sided, Freudian-inspired, and hence not especially open to a person's transcendental dimension. But, of course, there are excellent therapists, and if you look you can usually find one.

To be able to distinguish between psychic and spiritual is especially necessary when we have to deal with persons who think they have had extraordinary experiences. Even here, one should avoid extremes. To refuse everything as the products of fantasy would be as unwise as to naively believe that everything comes directly from God. Saint John of the Cross smiles at those who constantly believe they hear God talking: "God has said this or that to me." Of course, this happens, but less often than one thinks. In certain cases, it is completely impossible to decide with certainty whether the vision, revelation, or speaking is born of fantasy or comes from God. But that doesn't matter. Saint John of the Cross gives an extremely simple rule: Don't attach any weight to this; if the thing comes from God, it will in any event have its full effect, whether one believes it or not.

A spiritual guide, then, need not brood over whether an extraordinary experience is real or false. The best thing to do is not make too much noise about it, not speak too quickly about "great gifts of grace," and to return to the essential, which is to live in love for God and fellow man.

The interesting thing with prayer methods inspired by oriental meditation is that they affect the three levels of a person simultaneously.[22] The body feels better, one becomes psychically more "centered" and attains serenity, and in the spirit man opens himself to God. The ideal is that a spiritual guide deals with the whole person and helps him to develop on both the psychic and the spiritual plane. To build an intensive spiritual life on a fragile psyche carries great risks. Either the psyche collapses after a while under the spiritual pressure, or one begins to interpret one's psychic difficulties as mystical tests. Everything becomes transformed into mystical "night."

In *The Night Is My Light*, I have pointed out that psychic suffering *can* be a "night," depending on how someone takes his suffering.[23] It does not happen automatically and it presumes a large dose of humility. If the person in question gladly and often talks about his "night," it is suspect.

There is moreover, as I have suggested in the same book, a *real* and a *false* psychic suffering. Real psychic suffering is a consequence of the fact that the fundamental need for security, meaning, and love has not been satisfied. False psychic suffering, on the other hand, means that one flees from the real suffering. And the most common flight path is to project one's own disappointment, one's own revolt and guilt on others. Instead of letting God heal the wound, and little by little see that the love actually never was understood as if God was always present, one instead blames others. One wants others to change themselves, but doesn't want to take a single step.[24]

It is an illusion to believe that progress on the spiritual way always goes parallel with progress on the psychic way, or that God in the end will heal all psychic ailments. As a rule, a growing spiritual health affects the psyche in a positive way also (aside from certain crises of maturity which can mean a difficult burden for the psyche). But it doesn't mean that one becomes completely harmonious on the psychic plane. Even with a spiritually mature person some psychic "ailments" can remain. But he doesn't call them such. He experiences them not as a threat or as something which darkens God's light in him. They are completely accepted and integrated into his personality. They belong to his identity, like Jesus' *stigmata* after his Resurrection belong to his identity.

To Make a Virtually Decisive Decision

There are special situations where spiritual guides often are asked for advice and where their capacity for discernment is tested to an especially high degree.

What do we do when a young person comes to us and says, "I don't know whether I shall get married or go into the cloister. I believe that I have a calling, but I'm not certain." In earlier times, many Catholic Father Confessors had a ready reply to this question: "To take holy orders is better than to get married. Clearly, you should go into the cloister." Many priests even knew precisely which cloister the young woman should enter. The result was that, alongside many authentic callings, there were also candidates for the cloister who didn't belong there and became unhappy.

In our time, we don't believe that a Father Confessor or spiritual guide has a reply to this question. It is the one who asks the question who has the reply within him. What we can do is to deliver the answer, to help the confidant become conscious of the answer that she has deep within her.

A calling to the priesthood or to an order consists of three elements which can be expressed in this way: I *can*, I *will*, I *have to*. The same criteria can be used in most cases when a person asks God's will for his life. For a Christian, the choice of a life path is always an answer to God's calling. But the calling can be especially pronounced when it is a matter of deciding for a life wholly devoted to God. For this reason, my examples here are the callings to be a priest or nun.

We can help the candidate to research whether these three elements are present.

Can he: Does he have sufficient physical health, psychic balance, or spiritual maturity? Does the candidate really *want* it, or is it only a question of dithering? And *may* he: Is there a cloister or a bishop who is prepared to accept the candidate? It happens time after time that someone comes to us and says, "I have a calling to Carmel." We should then try to explain that one can be called to Carmel only if there is also a Carmelite cloister willing to open its gates.

When it concerns elements one and three, the same guide can often give a clear answer: He can evaluate the candidate's capacity and the likelihood that he will be accepted. But when it turns on element two, it is only the candidate who can reply. Only he can know whether the will is there. "If you wish…," says Jesus (Matthew 19:21).

To press someone by saying that God wants it is always wrong. God respects man's freedom. But we can help the candidate by patiently listening to him and letting him explain why he thinks he has a calling to the priesthood or to an order. By listening, we help the other to listen more to his own heart and get a clearer insight into his motives. Only by letting the candidate tell about his motives, an inner clarity grows within him. When he hears himself speak, he understands perhaps that some of his motives are superficial, childish. Through our questions, we awaken insight.

It can happen that we very well know what

would be best for those who seek our advice, but it is wise not to be too eager. The confidant himself should find out what is good for him. God's will is always "good" for man. When it concerns an authentic calling, the candidate always has a sense that this life will make him happy, that he will be in his own element, and will feel at home. One chooses a special life's path because one wants to obey God's calling, but also so that one will be happy. It is always a combination of both elements. If there was only obedience and no happiness at all, the calling is suspect. And if there is happiness and no pain caused by the fact that one must sacrifice something, the calling is similarly suspect. Often this is a good sign that the candidate's yes is the fruit of a more or less long struggle with God. If this struggle has not preceded the definitive decision, it usually will come afterward, and then the outcome is particularly uncertain.

If one compares the monastic life with marriage, one can say that it is more difficult to *go* into the cloister than to get married, but it is easier to *be* in a cloister than to be married. The very step into the calling can cost blood and tears, but once you have taken the step, you are ordinarily happy. It functions this way for the most part on the spiritual way: To come over a new threshold demands an extra effort and can feel difficult, but once one has passed over the threshold, everything goes easier, the air is cleaner, and one feels more free. To yield to "inclination" and "disinclination" is, on the other hand, easy to begin with, but afterwards one feels heavy and dissatisfied.

The point of departure for the person who is faced with a life-decisive decision must be that it is God's will and not his own superficial will one should aim to follow. It is to this point of departure we should try to guide our confidants if they have not already reached it. The fundamental question we should confront them with is: "What is the most important thing in life?" Perhaps we cannot always pose the question directly, but we can do it indirectly, and step by step, work our way forward to it. Sooner or later, the reply has to be that the most important thing is to do God's will.

Difficulties in Prayer

Nothing is so simple as to pray—to pray is to breathe—and nothing is so difficult, because we have become so complicated. One of the most common laments a spiritual guide can hear is: "I cannot pray any longer." The very formulation reveals that one thinks that he has been able to pray. Prayer has been, if not easy, in any event possible, and now it has become impossible. Every person who prays is sooner or later confronted with this impossibility.

How do we react as spiritual advisors? It *can* happen that the impossibility of prayer depends on the fact that life is not consistent with prayer. For someone who, during the day, is not at all concerned with God, it feels a little false during the prayer to say, "O how I love you, my God!" You don't need much discernment to be able to diagnose this gap between prayer and life.

That prayer becomes difficult depends often on something quite different. God invites us to a new way of prayer, and the person persists in trying to pray as he has always done. This disharmony between God and man inevitably creates discomfort. One has a certain idea of how the prayer should look. If the prayer no longer corresponds to the idea or ideal, one becomes unhappy and thinks that he no longer is able to pray.

But a prayer which is living is always a dynamic occurrence. It must be allowed to develop. It is the spiritual guide's job to show that it is not a bad sign when the old way of praying no longer works. She must explain that God now wants one to associate with him in another way. She can make clear that a prayer which really is a prayer, which is love, always has a disposition to develop from plurality to unity, from many words to few words or silence, from the superficial to the profound, from activity to passivity.

The development of the prayer is an "internalizing process." God wants man to find him at deeper and deeper levels of his essence. In the beginning, it's fine to meet him on the emotional level—in Saint John of the Cross' terminology: on the plane of the senses. But eventually God withdraws to a deeper level; he is no longer accessible on the periphery (the night of the senses). If you continue to look for him there, you will get *unmistakably* a feeling that the prayer has become impossible. But prayer *is* possible on a deeper plane. It is enough to relinquish self-importance and give oneself over to God. It is now God himself who, to a degree, takes over the prayer. From having been a subject, man now becomes an object. Here he finds perhaps no strong emotions but peace, instead.

When the confidant thus desperately questions, "But what shall I do?" the answer is: "Nothing! Let God do it! Learn to talk and think a little less and listen a little more."

It is true that in these simple prayers, one can be a bit unfocused, since one no longer has concrete points to be occupied with. For this reason, it can be good to repeat often prayer words ("Come, Lord Jesus," "Abba, Father," "Jesus") in order to keep conscious openness to God. But time after time, the guide must point out that the prayer in the first place does not deal with concentration. Concentration has to do with the head, while prayer is an affair of the heart. It is the basic setting of the heart it depends on. The will to be at God's disposal, to let him do what he will. And what he will is always: to love.

Then there *can* come a time when even this simple prayer becomes difficult, when one no longer experiences peace. God has pulled himself back still deeper into the center of the soul (the night of the spirit). Then, it is a matter of holding out in naked belief, that is to say, belief without any notable experiences.

Here takes place the Copernican revolution: Instead of letting God revolve around me—God for me—I begin now to revolve around God—I for God. One learns the pure love, agape; the old person dies and the new person stands up.

A spiritual guide ought to know something about this development. If he doesn't understand what is happening, he can scarcely support and console those who are going through the dark periods. And there are in fact more of them than you think who are doing it.

To Discern God's Will

A spiritual advisor also needs the ability to discern in order to teach his confidants to act as Christians. We act as Christians when we act like Christ, in obedience to the Father.

We can obey the Father only when we know his will. Many are bothered by the feeling that they never know the will of God. We have already talked about life-decisive decisions. Here, however, is more a matter of decisions concerning life's small details (but the details can, of course, be quite important): When shall we get up in the morning, how much time shall I devote to prayer, what do I do with TV watching, how do I fulfill the Church's teaching about fasting? What does God want? Such questions *can* indicate a pedantic mind, which as a rule is not difficult to recognize. But it can also indicate an honest attempt to live according to God's will.

We must look out in order to reply authoritatively to such questions, in order to stipulate what God wants. The confidant must himself find the answer. But we can be reminded of some criteria that can be helpful.

> God wants what suits *you*, what makes *you* well, and with *you*, I mean the entire you, thus both the body, psyche, and spirits. If God wants you to do something, he will create also the necessary conditions for this. He gives you healthy time, and even an inner longing and impulse, so that you can do this with a certain joy. If your fasting gives you a headache so that you do worse work, it is not God's will that you should fast in just that way. For a spiritual guide to say indiscriminately that one cannot go farther without a half hour's meditation every day is not judicious. Every person has his own "measure." The spiritual tradition speaks of *metron* (Greek) or *mensura* (Latin).

God doesn't demand the same thing of all. And what was right for me yesterday is perhaps no longer right today.

There was a time when one associated God's will with sacrifice. The more difficult something was, the greater the likelihood that it was God's will. It was a matter of forsaking my own will in order to do God's will. "Agere contra!" Of course, but *what* shall one act against, which "own will" shall we forsake? We must distinguish between the deep will and our superficial wills, or desires (what Saint John of the Cross calls "apetitos"). It is a matter of forsaking our superficial desires which we in our innermost know make us neither happy nor free.

To let yourself be led by the famous pair, "I like-don't like," turns a person into a slave. But our deep will, which is the organ of love, we should not forsake. And this deep will doesn't always lead us to "difficult" things, except maybe in the beginning and in testing times. Quite the contrary. Following my deep will causes me to bloom, both as a human and as a Christian. For those who seek God's will, the question is, "What do I want in my innermost inner?" The precondition is naturally to have learned the difference between "superficial" and "innermost inner."

André Louf expresses this in his already cited book on *apopthegma* (adage) from the tradition of the desert fathers, which in a fine way illustrates that we should respect each and every one's personal measure. In order to understand the anecdote, one should know that, among the desert fathers, there was a controversial question as to whether manual labor (to weave baskets, work in the garden) was compatible with a strict contemplative life. The strict school, to which Abba Poemen belonged, thought that such work disturbed the unceasing prayer. A brother came to Abba Poemen and said to him: "I sow my field, and the harvest I use to do good." "You do well," said the Abba to him, and the brother went his way encouraged and increased his charity.

Abba Anub happened to hear what Abba Poemen had said and questioned him: "Don't you fear God? How could you speak in such a way to the brother?" But Abba Poemen remained silent.

Two days later, Abba Poemen saw the brother come and said to him while Abba Anub could hear, "What was it that you said to me the other day? I didn't hear you properly." The brother replied, "I said that I sow my field, and the harvest I use to do good." Abba Poemen said to him, "I thought that you were speaking about your brother, who lives in the world. If it is you who are doing it, it's not suitable for a monk." When the brother heard that, he became sorry and said, "I cannot do any other work, and I cannot refrain from sowing my field."

When he had gone on his way, Abba Anub did metanoia (threw himself prostrate) before Abba Poemen and said, "Forgive me."

Abba Poemen said, "I knew also from the beginning that this was not work for a monk but I spoke according to the brother's way of thinking and gave him courage to continue with his charity. Now he has gone his way sorry and he will continue as before."[25]

Abba Anub's bad advice, given through Abba Poemen, made the brother sorry, depressed, and troubled. The brother knew that this advice didn't suit him, that he was in no position to follow it. This brings us to the second criterion: a thought, an impulse, that makes us unhappy, depressed, and dispirited does not come from the Holy Spirit. Or, positively formulated: An impulse or a plan that comes from the Spirit usually creates *peace*. "Let me hear what God the Lord will speak, for he will speak peace to his people" (Psalm 85:8).

When Saint Benedict in his Rule talks about fasting time and that the brothers then should do a little extra penance, he points out that this should take place "voluntarily and *in the Holy Spirit's joy*" (Chapter 49, 6).

Ignatius of Loyola in his *Spiritual Exercises* has given a detailed description of how a person can know whether a thought, a feeling, or an impulse comes from the good or the bad spirit. He gives eight rules "to more accurately discern the spirits." The most important rule is the first: "It is characteristic of God and his angels that in their movements are awakened true joy, spiritual happiness, the expulsion of all sorrow, and the bewilderment which the enemy brings" (329). Of the other rules, it is clearly wise to show a little patience and see whether this joy and happiness are lasting. Only when peace *lasts* can we be certain that we are in harmony with God's spirit.

The more a spiritual guide himself lives in accord with the impulses of the Spirit, the easier it becomes for him to recognize the work of *the Spirit* in the persons who trust in him. One can talk about a spiritual taste or perception (*aisthesis*) which can be developed and which can be finer and finer. Why should we otherwise pray: "Make me to know your ways, O Lord; teach me your paths"? (Psalm 25:4).

The Typical Christian Way of Acting

To act as a Christian means not only to do as God wills, but also to do it in the way he wills. There is a typical Christian way of acting. If we ourselves have learned this way, it will rub off on our confidants.

The Christian way of acting has two degrees. The first turns on acting not egocentric but theocentric, not for one's own sake but for God's sake. We can do wonderful things, but if we do them to show off, to be liked, to harvest gratitude, to earn money, to obtain a little more self-esteem, we cannot really talk about Christian behavior. The tensions which often prevail in devout societies and associations or among those who engage themselves in the congregation show that one does not always work "for God's kingdom," but for one's own "kingdom." There can be a lot of appetite for power in a church commitment.

It is our job as spiritual guides to contribute

to a growing insight in our confidants, insight into selfish motivation. Not by squarely saying, "You are doing this for your own sake," nor by discussing (discussion seldom leads to anything), but by careful questions or by our silence, our questioning silence.

The most important thing in life is not what one *does* but *why* one does it. In one or another way, this question must time after time be raised: "Why are you doing this, what do you actually want?"

In the old times, one taught Catholic children to say in their morning prayers that they would do everything "to the greater glory of God." This was fine. But maybe one did it a little too easily. It is not by saying this in the morning that one actually acted "to God's greater glory." There is required a great inner consciousness and a constant transformation.

The second degree is based on the idea that it is no longer I who act without God, but God who acts through me (cf. Galatians 2:20). "My Father," says Jesus, "is still working, and I also am working" (John 5:17). It comes again as a refrain in the Gospel according to John that the Son receives everything from the Father. "[T]he Son can do nothing on his own, but only what he sees the Father doing; for whatever the Father does, the Son does likewise. The Father loves the Son and shows him all that he himself is doing..." (John 5:19–20; cf 5:30, 12:49–50).

To act in a Christian way is to act as Jesus Christ did, that is, let the Father act through us. I am now no longer God's assistant, so that God does a part and I do another part. I "help" God by being released through God's own actions. What I do is no longer a work *for* God, but a *work of God*.

But is this not mystical? Yes! This is what the mystical is: that I live God's life more than my own, or in the words of Saint Thomas Aquinas when he spoke about the Holy Spirit's gifts, *Magis aguntur quam agunt* (they become acted upon rather than acting themselves). One is more passive than active. We need not be so afraid of the mystical. It belongs to the Christian life. Without the mystical, the Christian ethic doesn't function. I will remind you of Karl Rahner's (1904–1984) already famous words: "Tomorrow's Christian will be a mystic or, in general, not be."

There would be more of the mystical in the Church if we priests and spiritual guides dared aim a little higher in our pastoral work, which we naturally can when we, for our own part, in our own life, dare to set the goal higher. I have myself often observed that people are especially open and interested when they speak about this: that there is a way to act which is much more "I-less," passive and tranquil, because we are released through God's own actions. People understand this and do not think at all that it is so mysterious.

Such a way of acting is directly contrary to our inborn activism, which often is a flight from our inner chaos. It is only possible when we are totally carefree. One is not anxious, not restless for what the result will be. One gives oneself and one's capacity to God; then things will be as they will be. Such a freedom from care is not a lack of *engagement* and not a threat to the "quality" of the work. On the contrary, when worry about the result falls away, a quantity of energy is liberated which earlier was invested in fear. Only now is one totally available, usable.

If we want to teach our confidants to act in this way, we must teach them to become conscious of their stress. Stress means that one will do the thing oneself, instead of placing it in God's hands.

We must again and again point out that life

can be simpler and easier than what one often makes it, that we *can* let go of ourselves and our ambitions, that we can relax and take it easy.

"Commit your way to the Lord; trust in him, and he will act" (Psalm 37:5).

Epilogue

The spiritual journey that we were entrusted to support and encourage is nothing that should be *construed*. It is more a matter of helping the confidants to *discover* what they already bear within themselves. The guide's task is never to create anything new, but to *liberate* the resources which the Creator laid down in this particular person. It is important that he has, and makes use of, knowledge, insights, and earlier experiences. But he can never follow a pre-arranged timetable for his confidant. The meeting between the confidant and the guide is a living and mutual seeking after God, right here, right now.

When we accept someone for a spiritual advising session, it is always an invitation to ourselves to get closer to God. Our own inner journey goes farther if we place ourselves at the disposition of those who seek us. In the seeking of advice, it is God who calls us to a deeper giving out of ourselves and to greater openness for his leading of our lives.

The meeting with our confidants is not only a preparation to deepened contact with God, either for them or for us. It is in itself a special presence of God. When two persons in honest desire to find God and his intentions converse with each other, God reveals himself. The divine Word which dwelled among us has said, "For where two or three are gathered in my name, I am there among them" (Matthew 18:20).

There is something mystical in the spiritual advising conversation, which can be more or less tangible to the extent that we are open to the Spirit.

Spiritual advising is always a spiritual adventure.

Notes

1. *Pastoral Constitution on the Church in the Modern World*, 36.
2. Teresa of Ávila, *Book of My Life*, 13, 16, Karmeliterna, Tågarp Glumslöv, 1980, p. 102.
3. Saint John of the Cross, *Living Flame of Love*, 3, 30, Karmeliterna, Tågarp Glumslöv, 1984, p. 92.
4. Anthony Bloom, "The Goal of Care for the Soul" in *What Is a Man?* Pro Veritate, uppsala, 1973, pp. 97–98.
5. *Book of My Life*, 23, 8–9, p. 170.
6. Twenty-sixth Sunday during the year, Collect prayer.
7. André Louf, *Grace Can Do More*, Desclée de Brouwer, Paris, 1992, pp. 60–65.
8. Teresa of Ávila, *The Way of Perfection*, Kap. 4, 13, according to Escorial manuscript.
9. Thérèse of the Child Jesus, *Autobiographical Writings*, Karmeliterna, Tågarp Glumslöv, 1971, p. 40.
10. Saint John of the Cross, *Dark Night of the Soul*, I. 4, 7, Karmeliterna, Tågarp Glumslöov, 1972, p. 38.
11. Julian of Norwich, *Revelations of Divine Love*, Artos, Skellefteå, 1991, p. 88.
12. Owe Wikström, *The Blinding Darkness*, Libris, Örebro, 1994, p. 84.
13. *Autobiographical Writings*, p. 232.
14. Ibid., pp. 232–233.
15. Saint John of the Cross, *The Ascent of Mount Carmel*, I 13, 7, Karmeliterna, Tågarp Glumslöv, 1978, p. 71.

16. cf. Johann Baptist Metz in the article "Talk About God vis-à-vis the World's Story of the Passion " in *Signum,* 1993, 1, p. 19: "Was Israel happy with its God? Was Jesus happy with his Father? Does religion make anyone happier? Does it make anyone more mature? Does it provide identity? A home, security, peace with ourselves? Does it calm anguish? Does it answer questions? Does it fulfill desires, at least the most intense ones? I doubt.

    "Ask Mother Teresa, ask sisters, who more than any others live in close contact with 'the world's passion story,' whether God makes them happy! Ask the mystics. And the Psalms: 'Whom have I in heaven but you? And there is nothing on earth that I desire other than you' (73:25). There are, of course, cries of complaint and protests in the Psalms, but they are unable to nullify the dominant impression that God is our happiness."

17. Teresa of Ávila, *Interior Castle,* I, 1, 1 and 2, Karmeliterna, Tågarp Glumslöv, 1974, pp. 22–23.
18. Tito Colliander, *The Ascetic's Way,* Ortodox Kyrkotidningens förlag, Stockholm, 1973, p. 41.
19. *Catechism of the Catholic Church,* nr. 27.
20. *Revelations of Divine Love,* p. 69.
21. Ibid, p. 87.
22. cf. My book, *Eternity in the Midst of Time,* pp. 63–68. Relaxation prayer, breathing prayer, the whole reiteration.
23. In my book, *The Night Is My Light,* Karmeliterna, Tågarp Glumslöv, 1990, pp. 70–75.
24. Ibid, pp. 71–72.
25. *Grace Can Do More,* pp. 206–207. *Ökenfädernas tänkespråk,* översatt av Per Beskow, Artos, Storuman, 1982, pp. 113–114. (*The Proverbs of the Desert Fathers.*)